GEORGE NELSON

THE KING'S BUDGET

CONTENTS

First and Foremost I would like to dedicate all of my heartfelt praises to my heavenly father, Jesus Christ. The one who had my back all the way from the beginning many years ago. The one who called me into HIS PURPOSE when I refused to listen and obey. The one who put me through the fire, but never consumed of it. The one who pushed me into being uncomfortable to show me how to be comfortable again. The one who brought people in my life for a season, to teach me life lessons for a reason. The one who taught me how to survive in times of despair and heartache. The one who never gave up on "Me" throughout it all from brokenness to blessings, Jesus is the Reason for The Season.

Secondly, I dedicate my deepest love, loyalty and commitment to the love of my life, and 1st lady Ms Barbara Regeana Taylor. My hero, My Soulmate, My Best Friend. Thank you for all of your moral support in my journey of Purpose and Seeking to "Make A Difference" in the world. You have displayed day by day what a Woman of God looks and feels like in *"Real life"*. I am forever grateful and blessed to have you in my life everyday. I thank you for all the late nights and early mornings *"Without Complaint"*. I love you!

To the Bennett Family, Thank you for sharing with me your love, respect and acceptance into your family in every way. I shall take good care of your daughter as Christ loves the Church!

To the State of Georgia, (Georgia Department of Corrections) Thank you for putting me through the Georgia Penal System for if it was not for my incarcerated experience of many years, God's work in me would not be complete. Thank you for allowing me to "See the need, and fill it". To God be the Glory.

Last but not least, I want to Thank all the transitional programs, re-entry systems and half-way houses for returning citizens such as; Safe House Ministries, The Samaritan's House, A.C.S.S. , Atlanta Union Mission, The Y.M.C.A and Valley Rescue Mission for granting me the support I truly needed at the time. Your basic TLP programs added value to the Next Phase of My Life. Thank you for your support.

 First Printing, 2026

The King's Budget

CHAPTER

1

MEN SAVE, BOYS SPEND

REENTRY ACADEMY BUDGET (1)

Introduction

1. WHEN I WAS A BOY ...

2. GROWING UP AS A TEEN ...

3. DEVELOPING INTO MANHOOD ...

4. STANDING MY GROUND ...

5. FOCUSING ON MY FUTURE ...

6. LET'S GET TO WORK!

God says,

" For I know the plans I have for you, plans for your well-being, not for disaster, to give you hope and a FUTURE". CSB

APPLY THESE SCRIPTURES TO YOUR SAVINGS PLAN STUDIES AND WATCH GOD WORK!

- LUKE 16: 1-15
- 1 PETER 4:10
- PSALM 20:3-5
- 2 CORINTHIANS 5:17
- MARK 7:21-25
- PROVERBS 28:25
- ECCLESIASTES 4:8
- JOHN 15:5
- ACTS 19:5
- JAMES 4:13

For support email us: services@reentryacademy.org

WHEN I WAS A BOY

God's word: 1 Corinthians 13:11

"When I was a child, I spoke like a child, I thought like a child, I reasoned like a child, when I became a man, I put aside childish things". NIV

When you were a boy, how many times did you spend all of your money? $1.00, $5.00, $10 or even $20 dollars of your allowance money spent on things like; Games, Candy, Chips, Chewing Gum, Blow Pops, Amusement Park Rides, Cotton Candy and so many things around you as a boy in your neighborhood. And if you had friends, you did your best to find a way to spend your money on going to the movies, especially if you had a little girl who liked you too! It was inevitable sooner or later one of these things definitely had plans for your money, and you didn't even know it.

Statistics show that the average kid in a middle class family spends up to $2,331 US dollars annually. This has increased significantly since 1979 from $198 per year. With 31% of teens saving an average of $1,000 by the time they turn 18 years old. With the help and support of your parents, kids spend their money without a second thought of the FUTURE!

This is the mindset of a child.

1) What did you spend your money on as a boy?

____

2) Did you feel pressured to be like your friends? a) Yes: ____ b) No: _____

3) How did it make you feel when you didn't have money?

____

Notes: (List everything you remember that shaped your thinking about money as a boy)

____

____

____

GROWING UP AS A TEEN

God's word: 1 Timothy 4:12

"Don't let anyone despise your youth, but set an example for the believers in speech, in conduct, in love, and purity".

When you became a teenager, was your intentions with money pure? When we are young, we don't take the time to consider these things with money. Why? Because we can't see why purity and a clean heart has anything to do with how we manage it forward until it's too late. When I was a teen my parents didn't take the time to teach me about money and why my character matters. And just like many teens I fell short of producing good results early in my life (i just kept spending and spending like it grew on trees) SMH. Even when I started working and paying my little bills, I still didn't know how to save or even what to save for? The results were many lost opportunities to save my money and do something good with it.

4) What did you like about money as a teenager?

____

5) Did you change how you spent or saved money?

____

6) What was most important about money to you from 18-21 yrs old?

____

Notes: (List the new things you've learned about money from childhood to teenager)

____

DEVELOPING INTO MANHOOD

God's Word: Genesis 1:26

"Let us make man in our own image, according to our likeness. They will rule the fish of the sea, the birds of the sky, the livestock, the whole earth, and the creatures that crawl on the earth".

If you love money??? Don't believe The Hype!!! The **LOVE OF MONEY** is the root of all evil: And your precious temptations will keep your savings fund at "0" every single time. That's why growing from a boy with all kinds of high energy, eye opening spending opportunities to a level headed teen saving here and there will only get you to manhood...but it won't get you through MANHOOD. So the real question now is what?

What do we do with the real money we earn now? As men, we have major responsibilities...New job, New Wife, New Kids, New Car, New House and many bills. And this is just the beginning! I don't have to tell you, I have had all the above at multiple points in my life and have **LOST THEM ALL! It was easy to make money and spend it over and over again without SAVING when I was young and running the streets, BUT IT HURT MY FAMILY IN THE END.** Because I truly never learned how and why I should save for the future (*Shoot I was having a good time*) This was a hard lesson I will never repeat again. God said, we rule over the fish and the sea, but he didn't say do it foolishly.

7) When you became a man, how did you manage your money?

8) How many times have you started saving and ended up broke?

9) How many friends do you know spend more than what they have?

10) List family members that rely on your income to pay bills?

STANDING MY GROUND

STANDING YOUR GROUND IS GREATER THAN GOLD:

Many people have plans for your money, and many people come and go, but who STANDS THE TEST OF TIME is a man who is not afraid to take a STAND for HIMSELF. Your savings fund is the result of your hard work, smart thinking and love of thyself. For a man cannot help another without helping himself FIRST. This is God's Promise. *"For the love of Christ compels us, since we have reached this conclusion: If one died for all, then all died. And he died for all so that those who live should no longer live for themselves, but for the one who died for them and was raised". - 2 Corinthians 5:14-15 NIV.*

When a man saves for himself, he is saving for those who he loves. For savings is a clear indication of a man loving and supporting his family and those he truly loves. For a man's savings is a gift of wisdom God grants us to have as our own to build and prepare for challenging days ahead. This is true wisdom at its finest. **STAND YOUR GROUND, SAVE YOUR SOUL, SAVE YOUR MONEY!**

11) What challenges stop you from saving your money?

12) What are you willing to change?

____

____

13) How can you help someone else save money better?

____

____

____

14) What's your favorite scripture in the bible on money?

____

____

____

FOCUSING ON THE FUTURE

MEN SAVE, BOYS SPEND Is God's way of getting our attention in the early stages of life to prepare you for your future as you grow into a RESPONSIBLE MAN of God's Gracious Earth. No longer will I throw my money away, no more will I waste the treasures God has graced me with, and no longer will I turn away the value of **SAVING LIKE A GROWN MAN**. For we all fall short of God's glory, but when we learn better, we do better. AND NOW IT'S TIME DO BETTER AND TAKE UP MY CROSS AND WALK!

Let's discuss your new plans on SAVING MONEY GOD'S WAY. Review your answers above and let's pray over your new beginning and FUTURE SAVING PLAN. Fill out your spreadsheet attached and DO THE WORK!

CHAPTER

2

THE 50/50 PROMISE

Reentry Academy Budget (2)

Introduction

1. WHAT IS THE 50/50 PROMISE?

2. HOW DOES IT AFFECT MY SAVINGS?

3. WHEN CAN I APPLY IT?

4. DOES IT CHANGE OVERTIME?

5. WHY IS IT IMPORTANT?

6. LET'S GET TO WORK!

God says,

" Love the Lord your God with all your heart, with all your soul, and with all your mind".

This is the greatest and most important command. CSB

WHAT IS THE 50/50 PROMISE?

GOD'S WORD: 2 CORINTHIANS 9:6-9

"The man who sows sparingly will also reap sparingly, and the person who sows generously will also reap generously". Each man should do as he has decided in his heart - not reluctantly or out of compulsion, since God loves a cheerful giver. And God is able to make every grace overflow to you, so that in every way, always having everything you need, you may excel in every good work.

50/50 is what it takes to build your savings fund fast! When your money is flying out of your wallet faster than you can SAVE, it's time to excel your SAVINGS GOD's WAY!

50/50 means 50% EARNED 50% SAVED month to month guaranteed compounded monthly @ **600% for 12 months. THIS IS HUGE!** There is no other savings plan created to get your savings BACK ON YOUR FEET AGAIN like the **50/50 Promise!**

1) What do you expect the 50/50 promise to do for you?

____

____

2) Have you worked with a 50/50 savings plan before? a) Yes: ____ b) No: _____

3) How will it make you feel to save 50% every month?

____

____

Notes: (List the one thing you need to get done in the next 6 months)

____

HOW DOES IT AFFECT MY SAVINGS?

God's word: Psalms 119:9

"How can a man keep his way pure? By keeping his word". CSB

Throwing away your money is NOT KEEPING YOUR WORD. Throwing away your money is stopping your **SAVINGS FUND from DOUBLING!** When we run to the store for every immediate gratification we have, we SLOW DOWN OUR SAVINGS, When we just give without counting the costs, we SLOW DOWN OUR SAVINGS, When we allow friends and family to dictate what we need, we SLOW DOWN OUR SAVINGS, when we break the law of the land and have penalties or restitution to pay back, we SLOW DOWN OUR SAVINGS, when we consume far more the we SAVE, we SLOW DOWN OUR SAVINGS, and even when we support our families beyond our means...WE SLOW DOWN OUR SAVINGS!

When you start on your new savings mission, anything you spend outside of your plan, IS NOT KEEPING YOUR WORD. Because your word and God's Promise must be PROTECTED AT ALL COSTS. So that God can keep his promise through **"YOU KEEPING YOUR WORD".** This is how 50/50 will affect your savings!

4) When was the last time you used a budget?

____

____

5) What was the highest amount you ever saved?

____

____

6) Does anyone in your family manage money for you? Why?

____

Notes: (List the (1) thing that stop you from saving)

____

WHEN CAN I APPLY IT?

God's Word: PSALMS: 119:1-2

"How happy are those who keep his decrees and seek him with all your heart".

Remember when your parents saved their money to buy a house or a car:

Because back then, saving money was easier. We had less distractions, no technology and less spending habits. As a matter of fact, every time I earned my weekly $5 allowance, my mom would say; save your money boy, you never know when it's going to rain". So I would cut the neighbor's grass, and do extra errands to earn more money too. And before I knew it, I had $20 saved, but spent it going to the movies and bowling with friends. So I had to start all over again, SMH.

Before you start your new job, you can prepare your savings, or if you've been working you can start on your next paycheck. All it takes is a new shift of your mindset and let's Do The Work!

7) Are you good with saving money?

a) Yes: ____ b) No: _____

8) What was the most you ever saved before?

____

9) Do you have a closed checking or savings account? If yes, why?

____

____

10) Do you have direct deposit set up from your employer?

____

DOES IT CHANGE OVER TIME?

Your savings fund will continue to GROW AND CHANGE: And that's exactly what you NEED. The other good news also is that God's Foundation for your Savings Fund remains SOLID. As long as you have the discipline to go the course. God's savings promise will never change.

11) What challenges stop you from saving your money?

____

____

12) What character trait are you willing to change that may affect your savings?

____

____

13) How can you help someone else save money too?

____

____

14) What's your favorite scripture in the bible on money and stewardship?

____

WHY IS IT IMPORTANT?

1 Peter 5:11 You are guarded by God's power through faith for a salvation that is ready to be revealed in the last time. You rejoice in this, even though now for a short time if necessary you suffer grief in various trials so that the proven character of your faith - more valuable than gold which though perishable is refined by fire - may result in praise, glory and honor at the revelation of Jesus Christ.

God wants you to WIN! And your savings fund is living proof of his designed purpose in you. Let's discuss your new plans on SAVING MONEY GOD's WAY. Review your answers above and let's pray over your new beginning and FUTURE SAVING PLAN. Fill out your spreadsheet attached and DO THE WORK!

CHAPTER

3

THE GREATEST INVESTMENT

Reentry Academy Budget (3)
Introduction

1. **GOD DID IT**
2. **I DON'T DESERVE IT**
3. **FAMILY M.A.T.T.E.R.S.**
4. **TRASH vs TREASURES**
5. **THE GREATEST INVESTMENT**
6. **LET'S DO THE WORK!**

God says,

" Your wife will be like a fruitful vine within your house, your children, like young olive trees around your table, in this very way the man who fears the Lord will be blessed ". CSB

GOD DID IT

God's word: Romans 8:1-11

"Therefore, there is now no condemnation for those in Christ Jesus, because the law of the Spirit of life in Christ Jesus has set you free from the law of sin and death". CSB

Investing in others without understanding why God invested in YOU FIRST is like a tree being planted with **NO ROOTS.** You will fall and not stand the tests that come before you, you will not keep your word of managing your money God's way, you will not honor thy mother nor father, you will cause more grief for chasing money. Your sinful flesh will separate you from the gift of the spirit and the truth will remain hidden. Romans 7:14-15 *" For we know that the law is spiritual, but I am of the flesh, sold as a slave to sin. For I do not understand what I am doing, because I do not practice what I want to do, but I do what I hate" CSB.* This is the mindset of a Double Minded MAN. When a man desires to invest in himself he should repent and meditate on what God's plan is for **HIM FIRST.** For a man will not take good care of his family and the ones he loves without knowing the best investment in him is knowing that **GOD DID IT!**

1) What is the most powerful investment God can do for you?

____

____

2) Do you know how God's investment in you will work? a) Yes: ____ b) No: _____

3) What type of spiritual investment do you need to work on first?

____

Notes: (What do you believe God desires from you?)

____

____

I DON'T DESERVE IT

God's word: *"Whoever is faithful in very little is also faithful in much, and whoever is unrighteous in very little is also unrighteous in much. So if you have not been faithful with worldly wealth, who will trust you with what is genuine?* CSB.

GOD's INVESTMENT IN YOU IS MORE VALUABLE THAN SILVER and GOLD. No man earns grace; it is given unto us as God's Gift to do what is righteous among those who dwell among us. Many men have come and gone and have made a lot of money along the way, but how many men have taken the time to get closer to God's Grace and his Biggest INVESTMENT "YOU". There is no greater investment than this:

Ephesians 6:14-18

"Stand, therefore, with truth like a belt around your waist, chest, and your feet sanded with readiness for the gospel of peace. In every situation take up the shield of faith with which you extinguish all the flaming arrows of the evil one. Take the helmet of salvation and the sword of the Spirit - which is the word of God. Pray at all times in the Spirit with every prayer and request, and stay alert with all perseverance and intercession for all the saints". CSB

4) List family members you have invested in?

____

5) What type of spiritual return on investment have you accomplished?

____

6) Give a good example of God's spiritual investment in you...

____

Notes: (List all the new things you've invested in that yielded a good character return)

____

____

TRASH TO TREASURE

From TRASH to TREASURE is God's Ultimate Plan for Every Man. Many men fall short of God's Ultimate investment, but God is patient with us, and his timing is perfect. For all things are possible with Jesus Christ. When a man is broken, Christ investment guarantees a renewed sense of purpose, power and praise. A joyful sound of love, patience, compassion and hope overwhelms us. Our mind is clear, our thoughts are sound proof, our work is blessed, our family is blessed and anyone who enters our circle of influence. This is God's investment promise for all men who enter the kingdom of God and repent of his sins, throwing away old mistakes of the past to enter God's New Kingdom with many TREASURES.

Matthew 6:19-20

"Do not store up for yourselves treasures on earth, where moths and vermin destroy, and where thieves break in and steal. But store up for yourselves treasures in heaven, where moths and vermin do not destroy, and where thieves do not break in and steal. CSB

11) Do you have one of these? Jealousy, Envy, hatred, lack of compassion, cheating, etc.

____

____

12) Describe a time when your character bucket was filled with trash...

____

____

13) Name someone you know has a lot of character trash to empty out of their bucket...

____

14) How often did you take out the *"Physical Trash"* in your house?

____

THE GREATEST INVESTMENT

2 Corinthians 5:17

"Therefore if a man is in Christ, he is a New Creation. The old has gone, The New has Come" NIV

When we invest into ourselves, God reveals himself strong and mighty. When we allow God to turn our wrongs into rights, and when there's a new point of view based on our character we become stronger in obedience in every way.

15) How will you turn your character investment into God's new direction?

____

16) Who will benefit from your character investment most?

____

17) What plans are you putting into place for your family's future?

____

CHAPTER

4

THE BIG FOLLOW UP

REENTRY ACADEMY BUDGET(4)

Introduction

1. **THE BIG FOLLOW UP...**
2. **FOCUS ON PURPOSE...**
3. **SUCCESS IS IN YOUR HANDS...**
4. **ARMOR OF GOD...**
5. **LEAN NOT...**
6. **LET'S GO!**

God says,

He said to them, "Don't take money from anyone by force or false accusation, and be satisfied with your wages".

Luke 3:14 CSB

THE BIG FOLLOW UP

2 Corinthians 7:10

" For godly sorrow produces repentance *leading* to salvation, not to be regretted; but the sorrow of the world produces death ". CSB

God's Plan for you is to **DO IT BIG!** Because **BIG** Trials and **BIG** Tribulations call for a **BIG TESTIMONY** to share with the **WORLD.**

What's your follow up plan? Coming from all of your challenges, trials and tribulations you have a big testimony and story to tell men who are going through the same life experience as you. Whether it's drug abuse, alcoholism, lying, stealing, murder, imprisonment, we all have a testimony to share from brokenness. And who can be a better example for God More Than **YOU?**

1) ARROGANCE

Proverbs 8:13

"To fear the LORD is to hate evil; I hate pride and arrogance, evil behavior and perverse speech".

2) GREED

Proverbs 28:25

"The greedy stir up conflict, but those who trust in the LORD will prosper".

3) HATRED

Proverbs 10:18

"Whoever conceals hatred with lying lips and spreads slander is a fool".

4) SELFISHNESS

Philippians 2:3

"Do nothing out of selfish ambition or vain conceit. Rather, in humility value others above yourselves".

5) STUBBORNNESS

Jeremiah 7:24

"But they did not listen or pay attention; instead, they followed the stubborn inclinations of their evil hearts.
They went backward and not forward".

1) What's Your BIG FOLLOW UP PLAN? ____
____

2) Have you ever spent money arrogantly? a) Yes: ____ b) No: _____ c) Not sure: ______
3) Have you ever saved money selfishly?

____
____

Notes: (List everything God needs to change on how you think about money)

____
____

____

FOCUS ON PURPOSE

God's Word: Hebrews 12:2

"fixing our eyes on Jesus, the pioneer and perfecter of faith. For the joy set before him he endured the cross, scorning its shame, and sat down at the right hand of the throne of God".
CSB.

When We FOCUS... We give God our best, when we pray and meditate on his word we **SHOW GOD STRONG.** For our finances and money are not ours, it is the Lord's. And as Men of God we are chosen to be good stewards over our money. For when a man leaves this earth, he cannot take anything with him. For dust we arrive, and dust we shall return. "Have you ever seen a man take his possessions with him after death? The answer is a BIG NO! This is because no material in the world, nor silver or gold can replace the heavenly blessing of eternal life through Christ Jesus. **THIS SHOULD BE EVERY MAN'S FOCUS.**

Deuteronomy 5:22

"These are the commandments the LORD proclaimed in a loud voice to your whole assembly there on the mountain from out of the fire, the cloud and the deep darkness; and he added nothing more".

4) What is your Godly purpose?

____

____

5) How effective is God in your life?

____

____

Notes: (list issues you may encounter that will stop you from saving money God's way)

____

____

SUCCESS IS IN YOUR HANDS

God's Word: Joshua 1:8

"Keep this Book of the Law always on your lips; meditate on it day and night, so that you may be careful to do everything written in it. Then you will be prosperous and successful".

What tools are you using to support your Savings Plan?

6) Do you have scripture to support your plan? Yes: ______ No: ______ Maybe: ______

7) What is your idea of a SUCCESSFUL PLAN?

____

____

____

8) What is your FIRST STEP TO SAVE MORE?

____

9) What is your BEST SCRIPTURE ON MONEY?

____

PUT ON THE FULL ARMOR OF GOD.

***Putting on the Full Armor of God is Not for the WEAK* it's for the STRONG!** But not by might, but by spiritual STRENGTH that you FIGHT against the principalities of evil and the schemes of the enemy. For the devil comes to kill, steal and destroy every inch of a man's livelihood.

2 Corinthians 10:4-6

"The weapons we fight with are not the weapons of the world. On the contrary, they have divine power to demolish strongholds. We demolish arguments and every pretension that sets itself up against the knowledge of God, and we take captive every thought to make it obedient to Christ. And we will be ready to punish every act of disobedience, once your obedience is complete" NIV.

10) Share what you must do to combat the enemy schemes?

____

11) List friends who love money the way you did...

____

____

12) What money schemes do you see a pattern often in old friends?

____

____

13) List someone you know that will need help saving money too?

____

LEAN NOT...

Lean not on your own understanding, this is God's greatest saving commandment that will hold up his promise to you. For his word is more powerful than worldly wealth and great riches.

Exodus 31:3

and I have filled him with the Spirit of God, with wisdom, with understanding, with knowledge and with all kinds of skills—NIV

CHAPTER

5

BIG MOTIVATION

REENTRY ACADEMY BUDGET (5)

Introduction

1. **WHAT MOTIVATES YOU?**
2. **BE ENCOURAGED**
3. **F.ALSE E.VIDENCE A.PPEARING R.EAL**
4. **BIG MOTIVATION...BIG SAVINGS...BIG GOD**
5. **BIGGER IS BETTER!**
6. **LET'S GO!**

God says, Psalms 27:1-3

" The lord is my light and my salvation - whom shall I fear? The Lord is my stronghold of my life. Whom should I dread? When evildoers came against me to devour my flesh, my foes and my enemies stumbled and fell. Though an army deploys against me, my heart will not be afraid; though a war breaks out against me, I will still be confident".

WHAT MOTIVATES YOU?

Motivation comes from many sources...sex, drugs, gambling, the love of money, power and control and many things of the world that makes a man STUMBLE. It's hard to deny the many temptations men endure every day, but with God all negative motivations that hold us back are restored through the power of Jesus Christ. For he gave us his only begotten son as a living sacrifice that we may be saved through the confession of our sins, repentance and baptism that Jesus is Lord.

Genesis 35:11

And God said to him, "I am God almighty, be fruitful and increase in number. A nation and a community of nations will come from you, and kings will be among your descendants". NIV

1) What's Your MOTIVATION PLAN?

____

____

____

2) How often do you pray?

a) Daily: ____ b) Weekly: _____ c) Not sure: ______

3) What is the BIGGEST thing you've ever done?

____

____

Notes: (List 5 BIG SCRIPTURES YOU KNOW)

____

____

____

____

BE ENCOURAGED

Encouragement Starts with CHRIST...

Be alert, stand firm in the faith, be courageous, be strong, do everything in love.

When we encourage others we show Christ STRONG. When we SHOW CHRIST STRONG we allow his promise and word to change lives above ourselves. This process may not be easy, but well worth it in the end.

4) How may Christ encourage you?

____

____

5) List your favorite scripture here?

____

____

Notes: (list family members you would like to encourage)

____

____

____

F.ALSE E.VIDENCE A.PPEARING R.EAL

God's Word: 2 Timothy 6-7

"Therefore, I remind you to rekindle the gift of God that is in you through the laying on of my hands. For God has not given us a spirit of fear, but one of power, love and sound judgement". CSB

Fear is REAL... But only for MEN who believe in it. Since we know evil comes in many forms but only one purpose...to KILL, STEAL and DESTROY a man who has worked hard all of his life, yields the question, what else can a man utilize to rebuild his temple? For God gave us the opportunity to choose **FEAR or FAITH. And now it's all up to us to choose the right tools?...**

F.E.A.R. or FAITH

6) List the tools of FEAR according to the world?

____

7) List the tools of FAITH according to God?

____

____

____

8) What spiritual tools have you been using in your life?

____

____

____

9) What spiritual tools will you apply toward your savings?

____

____

BIG MOTIVATION. BIG SAVINGS. BIG GOD.

There's NOTHING BIGGER THAN GOD. "NOTHING". The Bigger The Problem... The BIGGER THE PRAISE!!!

Men have big problems many times in their life. But, how many take up their cross and GO BIG for GOD! You cannot fight a big problem with small prayers. If you command your mountain of problems to move, it will move on God's time. Your challenge is to find peace in the endurance of your struggle. For endurance yields good character as you rebuild over the strongholds you conquer as a new Man of God.

Luke 11: 10-13

"For everyone who asks receives, and the one who seeks the door will be opened. What father among you, if his son asks for a fish, will give him a snake instead of a fish? Or if he asks for an egg, will give him a scorpion? If you then, who are evil, know how to give good gifts to your children, how much more will the heavenly Father give the Holy Spirit to those who ask him? " CSB

10) What BIG Financial Problems do you have to conquer?

____

____

____

11) What BIG Prayers have you applied against BIG Problems?

____

____

____

12) Do you have a **WAR ROOM?** (a quiet space with God)

a) Yes: ________ b) No: _________ c) Not sure: __________

13) List your favorite WAR ROOM scripture here: ______________________________

BIGGER IS BETTER!

1 Corinthians 6:19

"Don't you know that your body is a temple of the Holy Spirit who is in you, whom you have from God? You are not your own, for you were bought at a price. So glorify God with your body". CSB

CHAPTER

6

SAVING BIG, INVESTING BIG

REENTRY ACADEMY BUDGET (6)

Introduction

1. **How BIG is BIG?**
2. **What does BIG mean to You?**
3. **B.I.G.G.E.R. Than LIFE?**
4. **What's the BIG DEAL?**
5. **Is God in your BIG PLAN?**
6. **LET'S GO!**

God says,

"But how can I bear your problems and your burdens and your disputes all by myself". CSB

HOW BIG IS BIG?

BIG PROBLEMS + BIG PRAYERS = BIG CHANGE

When men are determined to change for the better, that's when it's time to **PRAY BIG.**

God said,

" Simon replied, "I suppose the one who had the bigger debt forgiven, have judged me correctly", Jesus said ". **Luke 7:43**

1) Name a BIG DEBT YOU PAID recently?

____

2) How did it make you feel?

a) Thankful: ____ b) Appreciated: _____ c) The same: ______

3) Have you considered how big your prayers can affect other people?

a) Yes: ____ b) No: _____ c) Not sure: _______

WHAT DOES BIG MEAN TO YOU? BIG Debt can cause a Man to RUN

God says: *"The Lord is my light and salvation, whom shall I fear? The Lord is the stronghold of my life, of whom shall I be afraid? When the wicked advance against me to devour me, it is my enemies and my foes who will stumble and fall. Though an army besieges me, my heart will not fear; though war breaks out against me, even then I will be confident".*

Psalm 27: 1-3

4) How will you stand against BIG DEBT?

____

____

5) If your plan fails, what will you do next?

____

____

Notes: (list family members who need BIG PRAYER OVER THEIR FINANCES)

____

____

B.I.G.G.E.R. Than LIFE!

Believing In Greatness Gives Exceeding Rewards

God never gives Man more than what he can bear. Trials and tribulations are only for a season, the lesson in the trial is the REASON. When your prayers become bigger than your problems, your problems have no more room to grow.

6) List the problems that concern you...

____

____

7) List the BIG PRAYER that can defeat your problems...

____

____

8) What do you think it means to Repent, Repeat and Reserve?

____

What's The BIG DEAL? GOD is the BIG DEAL! And A Man's Savings is Attached To it!

Mark 7:20-23

"What comes out of a person is what defiles him. For from within, out of people's hearts, come ***evil thoughts****,* ***sexual immoralities****,* ***thefts****,* ***murders****,* ***adulteries****,* ***greed****,* ***evil actions****,* ***deceit****,* ***self-indulgence****,* ***envy****,* ***slander****,* ***pride****, and* ***foolishness****. All these evil things come from within and defile a person."* CSB

9) What is the BIG DEAL NOW? (Show an example of a Big problem for God...)

10) What do you think God commands of you?

11) What's your next BIG PLAN? Is God in the picture?

Is God In Your BIG PLAN?

Genesis 1:28

"God blessed them and said to them, be fruitful and increase in number; fill the earth and subdue it. Rule over the fish in the sea, and the birds in the sky and over every living creature that moves on the ground". **NIV**

CHAPTER 7

THE GIFT OF GIVING BACK

REENTRY ACADEMY BUDGET (7)

Introduction

1. Giving is G.R.E.A.T.E.R. 2. Why Give M.O.R.E.?

3. Taking (vs) G.I.V.I.N.G.

4. When Giving is Not Enough

5. Why God Gave Us Christ?

6. LET'S GO!

God says,

*"A generous person will be blessed, for he shares his food with the poor". **Proverbs 22:9 CSB.***

Giving is G.R.E.A.T.E.R!!!

When we are Greater...We allow Grace to Reveal Excellence Among Trials and Tribulations Every Resurrected Day of our lives!!!

That's why it's important to recognize God's presence when two or more gather. It is his purpose for men to achieve greatness in all areas of our lives. In family, friends, business; there's no place where GOD does not dwell. He gives us the choice to be greater than our circumstances. We know by his grace all things of the world are forgiven. This is revealed to each man through his trial and tribulation. And through your repentance your spirit is resurrected as a new man.

God said,

"The Lord passed in front of him and proclaimed: The Lord is a compassionate and gracious God, slow to anger and abounding in faithful love and truth" **Exodus 34:6**

1) Are You GREATER than your circumstance?

a) Yes: ____ b) No: _____ c) Not sure: _______

2) What does Greatness mean to you ?

3) What do you think Greatness have to do with YOU?

WHY GIVE MORE?

Giving begins with YOU Giving More To GOD.

God says: *"Give, and it will be given to you; a good measure-pressed down, shaken together, and running over - will be poured into your lap. For with the measure you use, it will be measured back to you."* ***Luke: 6:38***

4) What are you giving to GOD?

5) Why are you giving to GOD?

Notes: (list family members who you know need GOD too)

Taking (vs) G.I.V.I.N.G.

Taking from God is not the same as GIVING TO GOD. When we take from God we deny every blessing he shares with us and push him aside because of "SIN". Our flesh takes over and gives our flesh more credit than it deserves. It is not God's purpose for MAN to IDOLIZE HIMSELF. God instructs us to GIVE more than we TAKE.

6) Give an example of ways to give...

7) List ways the world takes from others...

8) What does it mean to Take Money vs Give Money?

When Giving is Not Enough?

God says,

"Moreover, I will give you what you have not asked for—both wealth and honor—so that in your lifetime you will have no equal among kings ". **1 Kings 3:13**

Did you not know you are part of a royal priesthood? God made you to rule over all the earth and every creature in it as likeness in his own image. This is a major responsibility MAN HAS BEEN GIVEN. That's why you must know..."**YOU ARE GOOD ENOUGH".** Don't allow the enemy a foot-hold in your spirit. Don't speak bad things into the atmosphere, nor deceive others to achieve things that do not exist. For the Lord's plan for your life is to love thy neighbor as your own body and give away all things of the world and FOLLOW HIM. This is GOD's Greatest Commandment.

WHY GOD GAVE US CHRIST? Christ is the Perfect Example of Sacrifice. The only one born of NO SIN. For this is God's Greatest Gift to MANKIND.

9) What is your greatest gift to give to the world?
(Show an example of a Great Gift you can offer God...)

10) How will your gift help others?

11) When will you put your gift into action?

CHAPTER

8

THE 50/50 CHECK UP

REENTRY ACADEMY BUDGET (8)

Introduction

1. **THE LOVE OF MONEY**
2. **GREED**
3. **SELFISHNESS**
4. **GOOD STEWARDSHIP**
5. **SELF CONTROL**
6. **DISCIPLINE**

Which term above will affect how you save money for the rest of your life?

____

(Expect to share your answer with the class...)

1) Do you know that your character has everything to do with you saving money?

a) Yes: ___ **b) No: ___** **c) Not sure: ___**

2) What stopped you from saving before?

____

3) How will you change your old savings habit?

____

4) Enter a Topic from the contents ____________________ and Let's Talk about It!

CHAPTER

9

MEN S.P.E.A.K.

REENTRY ACADEMY BUDGET (9)

Introduction

1. GOD
2. MONEY
3. TESTIMONY
4. FAMILY
5. FUTURE
6. GO GET EM KINGS!

"Start where you are...God will take care of The Rest"

"We need you to survive, We won't harm you with words from our mouths.
We need you to survive"
Reentry Academy Worldwide

90 Day Savings Evaluation

SAVINGS PORTFOLIO FOR: ____________	(30) Days	(60) Days	(90) Days	Savings Total
Self Employment / Flexible Hrs				
Full Time Employment (40 hrs)				

Part Time Employment (20 hrs)				
Commission Rate (per payroll)				
Over Time (extra earnings)				
Earnings and Income Total:				
Tithes and Offerings: (10%)				
MY NET INCOME:				
(50%) INCOME TOTAL				
EXPENSES PAID TOTAL				
Rent / Mortgage				
Food / Groceries				
Transportation / Bus / Uber Etc...				
Auto Expenses				
Utilities / Electric / Gas / Etc.				
Smart Devices in Household				
Hygiene / Health / Exercise				
Child Care Expenses				
Miscellaneous /				
Total Living Expenses:				
Total Savings Plan:				

CHAPTER

10

KING AMONG K.I.N.G.'S

REENTRY ACADEMY BUDGET (10)

Introduction

1. **We T.H.I.N.K.**
2. **We S.H.A.R.E.**
3. **We E.N.C.O.U.R.A.G.E.**
4. **We C.O.M.M.I.T.T.**
5. **We S.A.V.E.**
6. **We W.I.N!!!**

"Congratulations Kings!!! SAVE BIG

God says,

***"Therefore, there is now no condemnation for those who are in Christ Jesus"* Romans 8:1 NIV**

90 Day Savings Evaluation

SAVINGS PORTFOLIO FOR: ______________	**(30) Days**	**(60) Days**	**(90) Days**	**Savings Total**
Self Employment / Flexible Hrs				
Full Time Employment (40 hrs)				
Part Time Employment (20 hrs)				

Commission Rate (per payroll)				
Over Time (extra)				
Earnings and Income Total:				
Tithes and Offerings: (10%)				
MY NET INCOME:				
(50%) INCOME TOTAL				
EXPENSE SAVINGS TOTAL				
Rent / Mortgage				
Food / Groceries				
Transportation / Bus / Uber Etc...				
Auto Expenses				
Utilities / Electric / Gas / Etc.				
Smart Devices in Household				
Hygiene / Health / Exercise				
Child Care Expenses				
Miscellaneous /				
Total Living Expenses:				
Total Savings Plan:				

[RESOURCES]
Online Biblical resource: www.biblegateway.com
Open a free account for checking and savings accounts: www.Chime.com
Online child support services: Contact your state's department of human resources.
Online credit repair: Experian, Transunion or Equifax.
Online retirement resources: Search Roth IRA, 401K plans by employer etc.
Online starting a business resource: www.sba.gov
Online Job Search: Ex-Offender Jobs (Google)

- **The Kings Budget Workbook is created by the Reentry Academy Graduate Program for men seeking to get back on their feet God's Way. If you know of a family member or anyone who needs help please reach out to www.Reentry-Academy.org for community services, scheduled classes and workshops coming soon to a city near you.**

"For God knows the plans he has for you, plans to prosper you, not to harm you. Plans to give you a hope and a future" Jeremiah 29:10

WHO IS GEORGE NELSON?

A budget servant leader and re-entry coach for GOD. With 40 years of surviving the streets and attending the school of HARD KNOCKS, George Nelson has overcome 19 years of chronic homelessness, financial ruin, incarceration and re-entry experience he will never forget. Now he pays it forward to help men coming out of incarceration to SAVE BIG GOD'S WAY!

No more will you be treated as a criminal, no more will you be called a number, and no more will you be treated less than human. For every man shall now take up their cross and walk as "Kings" coming back in the community God's Way.

To book a coach at the Reentry Academy go to: www.ReentryAcademy.org online or call (423) 298-2139 Mon - Friday: 9am - 5pm. Classes and workshops are designed for returning citizens coming back into the community released from the courts, judges and pardon and parole boards seeking to take their reentry living lifestyle to the next level. We help with financial literacy workshops, next level budgeting to save for major purchases i.e. down payment on a house, new car, better credit, child support arrears, paying for college etc. We are reentry professionals who can help push your financial agenda forward God's Way.

Budgeting classes are consecutive (10) weeks at our location 9320 Lee County Road 240 , Phenix City Alabama 36870. For classroom hours please visit the website. Classes are $50 each, comes with A "King" Workbook, A Bible, A Budget Coach and Refreshments. Our mission is to take your savings plan TO THE NEXT LEVEL GOD'S WAY. To secure your space please register online @ www.ReentryAcademy.org

CALLING ALL...HALFWAY HOUSES, RE-ENTRY CENTERS, TRANSITION LIVING PROGRAMS, RECOVERY CLUBS AND CHURCH MINISTRIES PARTNER WITH US @ Reentry Budget Academy and help your community save money again!
You'll love it, We Promise!

BUDGET COACH OF THE YEAR
Brother George Nelson
www.ReentryAcademy.org

www.ingramcontent.com/pod-product-compliance
Lightning Source LLC
LaVergne TN
LVHW070955210926
848482LV00002B/222
* 9 7 9 8 2 9 5 6 3 0 7 4 3 *